6

Celebrating 40:
This is My Year!

A Green Shoe Press
Let's Celebrate: Hundred Pages Series
publication.

For information on other books or journals
in the Be Creative Series or Hundred Pages Series
or to request VJ Schultz as a speaker,
email: verasversion@gmail.com

Published April 2015

Printed by CreateSpace, An Amazon.com Company
ISBN-13: 978-1511661409
ISBN-10: 1511661402

Celebrating 40
in My Words

Dates:

From _____ *to* _____

If Found Please Call:

_____

The BIG One

Birthdays come and birthdays go;
Some are super special years.
40 is a BIG one so--
Count your joys, not your fears.

Inside empty pages wait,
Your thoughts to fill their blank state.
Enjoy the year! Laugh out loud!
Record what will make you proud!
--VJ Schultz

Suggestions for what to write inside your special book during your special year:

A bucket list of what you want to do, or new things to try between now and your next birthday.

What you do accomplish and your experiences doing so (include the facts: who, what, when, why, how, where).

The best things about being 40.

Your thoughts, experiences, friends, family, activities.

You could even ask friends or family members to add a memory of an experience you shared.

And whatever else you like because this is your book in which to record your special year.

Most Important Pages

_____	*Page___*
_____	*Page___*
_____	*Page___*
_____	*Page___*
_____	*Page___*
_____	*Page___*
_____	*Page___*
_____	*Page___*
_____	*Page___*
_____	*Page___*
_____	*Page___*
_____	*Page___*
_____	*Page___*
_____	*Page___*
_____	*Page___*
_____	*Page___*
_____	*Page___*
_____	*Page___*
_____	*Page___*
_____	*Page___*
_____	*Page___*
_____	*Page___*
_____	*Page___*
_____	*Page___*
_____	*Page___*

Made in the USA
Middletown, DE
03 April 2016